BOOK WORMS

OPPOSITES

Hot Cold

Apple Jordan

Marshall Cavendish
Benchmark
New York

Soup is hot.

Ice cream is cold.

Hot chocolate is hot.

Lemonade is cold.

An oven is hot.

A refrigerator is cold.

Fire is hot.

Ice is cold.

I am hot!

I am cold!

Words We Know

Soup

Ice cream

Hot chocolate

Lemonade

Oven

Refrigerator

Fire

Ice

Index

Page numbers in **boldface** are illustrations.

About the Author

Apple Jordan has written many books for children, including a number of titles in the Bookworms series. She lives in upstate New York with her husband and two children.

With thanks to the Reading Consultants:

Nanci Vargas, Ed.D., is an Assistant Professor of Elementary Education at the University of Indianapolis.

Beth Walker Gambro is an Adjunct Professor at the University of St. Francis in Joliet, Illinois.

Published by Marshall Cavendish Benchmark
An imprint of Marshall Cavendish Corporation

This publication represents the opinions and views of the author based on Apple Jordan's personal experience, knowledge, and research. The information in this book serves as a general guide only. The author and publisher have used their best efforts in preparing this book and disclaim liability rising directly and indirectly from the use and application of this book.

Other Marshall Cavendish Offices:
Marshall Cavendish International (Asia) Private Limited, 1 New Industrial Road, Singapore 536196 • Marshall Cavendish International (Thailand) Co Ltd. 253 Asoke, 12th Flr, Sukhumvit 21 Road, Klongtoey Nua, Wattana, Bangkok 10110, Thailand • Marshall Cavendish (Malaysia) Sdn Bhd, Times Subang, Lot 46, Subang Hi-Tech Industrial Park, Batu Tiga, 40000 Shah Alam, Selangor Darul Ehsan, Malaysia

Marshall Cavendish is a trademark of
Times Publishing Limited

Library of Congress
Cataloging-in-Publication Data

Jordan, Apple.
Hot cold / Apple Jordan.
p. cm. — (Bookworms. Opposites)
Summary: "Depicts familiar items that are hot and items that are cold to demonstrate the concept of hot and cold" — Provided by publisher.
Includes index.
ISBN 978-1-60870-409-5
1. Heat—Juvenile literature.
2. Cold—Juvenile literature.
3. Temperature—Juvenile literature.
4. Polarity—Juvenile literature.
I. Title.
QC256.J67 2012
536'.5—dc22   2010039539

Editor: Joy Bean
Publisher: Michelle Bisson
Art Director: Anahid Hamparian
Series Designer: Virginia Pope

Photo research by Tracey Engel

Cover: Tim Hale/Getty Images (left); Michael Kelley/Getty Images (right)
Title page: Melanie DeFazio/Shutterstock (left); Paula Hible/Getty Images (right)

The photographs in this book are used by permission and through the courtesy of: *Getty Images*: Mimi Haddon, 2, 12 (top); Paula Hible, 5, 13, (top, left); Bellurget Jean Louis, 8, 13 (bottom, right); Tom Morrison, 11. *Alamy*: RubberBall, 3, 12 (middle); moodboard, 7, 13 (middle, right). *Shutterstock*: Melanie DeFazio, 4, 12 (bottom); iofoto, 6, 13 (top, right). *iStockphoto*: Christopher Futcher, 9, 13 (bottom, left); Marilyn Nieves, 10.

Printed in Malaysia (T)
1 3 5 6 4 2